"If you want a great read with awesome advice on networking, then this book is a must on your book shelf. Sandy offers a truckload of practical 'how to' strategies, tips, insights, best practices and examples to illustrate her points. Her pay-it-forward approach is a revolutionary idea I found especially intriguing. If you're struggling for ways to expand your professional contacts and relationships, you'll find lots of answers in the pages of this excellent book."
Alan Collins, Author of 'Unwritten HR Rules' and former Vice President of Human Resources at PepsiCo

"Sandy Jones-Kaminski is the Supreme Queen of Networking, and has lots to teach the rest of us about how to network professionally in a truly effective way that also makes one's personal life richer, more meaningful and more fun. Buy her book, read it and then put her lessons to work to make you wealthy in contacts, opportunities, colleagues, and friends. Sandy's insights and philosophy help you understand how to approach networking in a fresh new way. Her tools and tips help you actually practice networking much more powerfully. For urban professionals seeking to grow their meaningful professional contacts, this book is simply a 'must have,' and if a Norwegian bachelor farmer read Sandy's book, and put it to use, he would be having a lot more fun at the Grange Hall and church suppers he has been too shy to attend."
Susannah Malarkey, Executive Director, Technology Alliance, Seattle

"Sandy Jones-Kaminski is a skilled networker, but with a unique twist: she knows how to motivate and inspire people to change their focus from Me to We. The result: a wide network of professionals who meet regularly to help one another. Most networking groups—and networkers—focus on ways to benefit themselves. Sandy is a master at gathering people who want to benefit all—and she does so in a very natural, laid-back way. Don't bother buying other networking books with the Me First mindset. The value of Sandy's approach and the tools she provides are far more beneficial, and frankly, more fun."
Eric Weaver, Account Director, Tribal DDB

"When it comes to networking, Sandy's book nails it. While the wake-up call has finally reached just about everybody in terms of the importance relationships play in business and career success, as she notes, and I've observed firsthand, you still find about 80% of the folks out there struggling to really 'get' the process or understand how to go about it effectively. For this crowd, Sandy's advice is invaluable. She breaks the entire concept of networking down into a series of easily digestible parts and then sprinkles in her own hard-won insights over how to build relationships that matter. Whether you're a rookie or an old pro at the networking game, I guarantee you'll walk away from this book with some new ideas, tools, and tactics that will help you be more successful!"
Matt Youngquist, President & Founder, Career Horizons, LLC

"This book is a unique and thoughtful approach to making you realize that networking is a part of everyday life. Sandy really simplifies the act of networking and makes it easy and actionable for anyone. It's the perfect quick guide for any college student or recent grad to learn the basics on how to approach and be successful in networking—and have fun doing it!"
Julie Ahn Goldthwait, former Vice President & General Manager, MonsterTRAK

"In our economic climate, the art of networking is a critical skill, and as a connector myself, I've seen many struggle to engage in meaningful conversation in casual business situations. In this networking primer, Sandy Jones-Kaminski succinctly and powerfully reminds us all of our responsibility to ourselves and to others as we navigate an ever-changing business environment. By embracing her pay-it-forward approach, you'll open up a world of opportunity—and valuable connections—that didn't seem possible before. And you'll be able to turn a dry business affair into something interesting and fun!"
Katherine Hall, Immediate Past President, Puget Sound/Seattle Chapter, American Marketing Association

I'm at a Networking Event—Now What???

A Practical Guide to Getting the Most Out of Any Networking Event

By Sandy Jones-Kaminski
Foreword by Courtney McKenzie

20660 Stevens Creek Blvd., Suite 210
Cupertino, CA 95014

First Printing: October 2009
Paperback ISBN: 978-1-60005-166-1 (1-60005-166-9)
Place of Publication: Silicon Valley, California, USA
Paperback Library of Congress Number: 2009938535

eBook ISBN: 978-1-60005-167-8 (1-60005-167-7)

Trademarks

Warning and Disclaimer

iv

Dedication

To my amazing husband, Keith Kaminski, my favorite wingman.

Acknowledgments

I would like to thank my husband, the artist still known as Keith Kaminski, not only for his unconditional love, support, and encouragement, but also for his inspired creation of the cover design for this book. He always manages to make my sometimes-harebrained ideas come to life, and then adds his own creative brilliance and we end up with awesomeness. I love you, babe. You are very special to me.

I'd also like to thank some of my friends and supporters for their encouragement, during the past 12 months: Maria, Stephanie, Julie, Stan, Annie, Siobhan, Courtney, Joan, Karin, Annie, Sima, Geoff, Susannah, Deanna, Ruth, Mary, Ann-Marie, Katherine, Matt, Ginny, Jeff and Alan. What would I have done without you? I also want to thank the many other wingmen (and women) who often accompany me as I network and connect practically everywhere I go. I appreciate their patience and collaboration as we go about exploring the world, because as they often experience with me, I find the people that inhabit it just as interesting as everything I learn, see, do, or hear.

It's very apparent to me that I wouldn't have even attempted to write this book, and tackle this particular topic, if it weren't for the initial nudges from John Kelly, a former co-worker of mine, when he made the suggestion that I author a white paper about networking (something I recommend to all would-be authors), and Lisa Crunick, a talented wellness professional, when she asked, "Why don't you just write an e-book about how to have one of your PIF Parties?" Both suggestions lead me to this book. And then, thank goodness for the folks at Happy About®, and especially Mitchell Levy, because after a fairly deep, but only twenty minute conversation, he expressed interest in publishing me and provided encouragement and the inspiration to help me see what was possible (something I usually do for others). Thanks also to the very talented Annie Laurie Malarkey (http://www.annielauriephotography.com) for the "just-right" new headshot, and the wonderful folks at InSpa (especially Shirene!) for helping me ward off carpal tunnel and making it possible for me to repeatedly sit at my laptop for hours at a time.

I also want to thank the hundreds of generous (and occasionally not so generous) people I've met through networking. Without them, I don't think I'd have nearly as much material as I have to write this book, and not nearly as many valuable insights to share with you. Thank you for the learning!

And last, but certainly not least, thanks to the rock stars that allowed us to turn their business cards into some of the business card people (BCP) at the imaginary networking event on the cover: Drew Banks, Curt Collinsworth, Aaron Fairchild, Julie Goldthwait, Mitchell Levy, Amanda Kezios at Mojo Spa, Shari Sewell, Eric Weaver and Jennifer Yost. I'd be happy to attend a networking event with any of you anytime.

A Message from Happy About®

Contents

Preface

As the principal consultant of Bella Domain, LLC, a business development strategy firm, and the recent VP of Networking for one of the largest chapters of the American Marketing Association, I have been told, on more than one occasion, that I know more than most about effective networking. In addition, and as the result of having built fairly robust personal and professional networks from scratch three different times in three different locations, during the past ten years, I have proven that I have the know-how and skills needed to make quality connections, cultivate relationships, host some great networking events, and create what I refer to as good "social capital."

During the past ten years, I have built networks in San Francisco, Chicago, and most recently Seattle, where partly due to a local phenomenon called the "Seattle Freeze,"[1] I was seriously motivated to do two things:

1. start hosting a casual networking event called a PIF (as in pay it forward) Party, and
2. volunteer to serve as the VP of Networking for a trade association of which I was a member.

---

1. Do a search on the term "Seattle Freeze" and you'll come across many explanations, but this one from the Seattle Times is pretty comprehensive – http://tinyurl.com/3wh7z seattletimes.nwsource.com.pacificnw/2005/0213/cover.html

As both a start-up and mature company vet, with experience as an executive in operations and strategic business development, I feel like I have seen it all when it comes to professional networking, and I also tend to spend time with the types of people who have seen what I may have missed. And, if all this experience weren't enough to make me somewhat of an expert, in various roles throughout my career, I have actually been told and paid to "just go network."

The reality is, no one actually teaches you these skills early in your career, or even while you're on the job. Mostly, you learn it by doing it, so let me share with you all my shortcuts, rules of thumb, some trial and error, and let's do some networking!

Foreword by Courtney McKenzie

Being in the presence of expert networkers at a social gathering, business event, or coffee meeting is an inspiring experience. Dynamic, conversational, glib...they seemingly pull ideas and connections out of thin air. Excited and engaged, they are constantly seeking to bring people together, quick to remember names, events, and places, and as they move through a room, they leave warmth in their wake.

People think that true networking is a gift that allows one to easily connect people, ideas, and resources. In truth, it's an acquired skill that anyone can develop with the right guidance. Everyone has the potential to develop their networking skills and no one person will network in exactly the same way. It's your unique personality that will define the nature of your networking style and drive your success.

In the past few years, social networking has taken on a personality all of its own, with the introduction of business and personal tools on the Internet such as LinkedIn, Facebook, MySpace, and Twitter. With 50% of America using these tools, it would seem that everyone is networking these days. But in truth, these tools take us further away from the art of personal networking; the face-to-face meeting of people for the first time, the nurturing of connections, and the building of circles of friends.

With 70% of all communication being non-verbal, nothing replaces the communicative value of face-to-face interaction over a glass of wine or a cup of coffee. Sandy reminds us to always seek out those valuable 15 minutes of in-person conversation (even when they seem intimidating) so that you can put the face to the name.

As a business development pro and expert networker in her own right, Sandy has not lost the skill of the face-to-face meeting, and in the following pages she reminds us of the lost art of hosting a social gathering for the purpose of networking—of how to bring individuals of like-interests together, actively engage them in a social setting, and draw them out from behind the false front of their computer screens.

Throughout these pages Sandy is going to take you back to the basics of social networking. She will point out that the elements for true networking are all around you, just waiting to be pulled together (by you!). She will teach you how to bring warmth, personality, and legitimacy to social interactions and that these personal connections, these extended communities, are what really define how we go through life.

Bottom line. Everyone has the ability to network and, thanks to Sandy, everyone now has the perfect tool to learn how. If you're reading this foreword, you're one of the lucky ones who now have Sandy as your personal networking mentor. Don't let her down, there's no excuse now not to learn how to network. Sandy has excitedly created a "How-To" Guide that reveals all the "secrets" of networking.

Thank you for bringing us all together, Sandy! Thank you for being so acutely aware of all the connections around you.

Courtney McKenzie
Email Marketing at Expedia, Inc.
LinkedIn profile: http://www.linkedin.com/in/courtneymckenzie

Introduction

I often describe myself as a networking enthusiast and believe that Malcolm Gladwell, author of 'The Tipping Point,' would likely identify me as a "Connector" and a "Maven."

In this book, I wish to illustrate that today's intense social networking environments practically demand that you have at least some knowledge of the best practices and effective tactics of networking, in order to achieve the results you are looking for from this potentially time consuming, yet very worthwhile, part of modern life.

For some, the contents of this book will serve solely as a reminder, but for many, it will offer some valuable insights on what to do, and just as importantly, what not to do while you're out there working hard to maintain good standing within your social networks (online or otherwise), and striving to grow and nurture your own valuable social capital. You'll also learn why you might want to consider becoming a "pay it forward" focused person, as well as how to be more memorable and thoughtful while putting forth all that effort.

And, while today, networking occurs as much online as it does offline (yes, you need to do both), we're not going to differentiate too much in this book, but it's worth mentioning that, as a general rule, it's always best that you don't do or say anything online that you wouldn't in person.

Let's Talk About Something First...

So, you went ahead and said yes, not maybe, to the invite you received for an upcoming networking event being hosted by your local "insert association/club/vendor name here." You received this invite via a forward from the same friend/mentor/coach/relative/boss who told you that you need to "get out there and network!" in order to find one or more of the following:

- A job
- Leads
- A mentor
- An agent
- A coach
- Recruiters
- New friends
- Clients
- Prospects
- Contacts
- Volunteers

Well, whether you're an extrovert or introvert, there are some best practices when it comes to approaching a networking event in a prepared and focused way. If it makes you feel better, you can call these rules, but whatever you call them, please try your best to mind them because after years of seeing all the ineffective ways people try to network, and simultaneously collect loads of stories regarding the crazy things people will do to get what they want, I knew it was definitely time to put it all in writing and share it with you.

And, coupled with my own motivations, with where unemployment rates are these days, and the record number of people that are out there trying their hand at networking in these desperate times, I'm worried that the effective networkers out there will start a secret society of "power networkers" that will only help each other in the years to come.

Personally, I keep finding proof that the Pareto principle (80/20) applies to networking best practices in general:

Twenty percent of the people truly get it, and then about 80% of folks don't. What I think happens is that the 20% of us are doing the majority of the power networking, and then acting like the "Connectors" (Gladwell/Tipping Point reference) we are, and pretty much doing all the heavy lifting for the remaining 80%.

If you are an aspiring power networker you probably think this is great, but I say that's only the case if you always want to be in that role, or are a full-time recruiter. I have seen proof that it is also not so good in that we're often only really networking amongst ourselves. I believe that the goal needs to be that the folks that "get it" must help the 80% out there see the light and continue to help show them the way. This is partly why I wrote a white paper on the topic of networking earlier in 2009 and what led to my writing this book.

Networking—an Introduction

I realize that I can't dig into this topic without first acknowledging that there exists some general anxiety, which many people feel when merely faced with an invite to a networking event, and in many cases with good reason. Heck, even some of us fearless types can also have that reaction because we have all too often been beyond frustrated with the outcomes of, and behaviors at, many of the networking events we attend.

At gatherings in Chicago, San Francisco, NYC, Silicon Valley, and now Seattle, I have frequently witnessed behaviors from the old "I'm talking to you, but try not to notice my eyes scanning every other person's nametag that walks by please," to the "So, Sandy what's Bella Domain?" And then the eyes glazing over because you, your situation, or words don't immediately appear to be a likely prospect for them. It's no wonder most people experience anxiety!

As many of us know, the joke is quite often on these shortsighted folks because, sometimes while we don't appear to be a prospect, our husband, sister, friend, cousin or co-worker just might be the type of decision maker with whom they really want or need to connect.

Quite a few years ago, I recognized that there had to be a better way to make and cultivate quality connections, so I'd rather unwittingly started taking the "paying it forward" approach to networking. I will attempt to share my knowledge here.

The Pay It Forward Approach

What's the pay-it-forward approach? Well, thanks to that movie with the kid from Sixth Sense in it, a lot of us understand that the expression "pay it forward" is used to describe the concept of asking that a good deed be repaid by having it done to others instead.

What this basically means is that you try to be attentive wherever you are, for opportunities to help someone else. What a novel idea, huh?

Perhaps you have an older co-worker who is too proud to ask for help with the shared login for the company Twitter account, or maybe you're at your company's open house event and see someone who looks like they could really use some insider introductions, hovering just past the entrance to the party. Well, the belief is that by helping either of these folks, you can quite possibly change people's attitudes about at least a little part of their world through your unobtrusive acts of kindness.

My favorite part of all this, and what I attempted to demonstrate at the Pay It Forward (PIF) Parties I've hosted, is that when a person thanks you and wants to "repay" you (that is, pay it "back"), let them know that what you'd really like is for them to pay it "forward"—you'd like them to do something nice for a few other people they don't know (my guests at my PIF Parties, for example), and ask those people to do something nice for a few more people. The idea is to make a conscious effort to increase the goodness of your corner of the world, and networking situations are the ideal environments in which to give it a go.

The Debate Is Over

There's little debate today that most of us should always be networking, and the truth is most of us actually are. We do it all the time—whether it's at a professional association's luncheon event, at a friend's wedding, at a church gathering, the senior center where we volunteer once a month, or the sidelines of a soccer field. Don't even get me started on how many people make new key contacts at their kids' sports event. (I admit it does make me think hard about adopting sometimes!) People can network or connect with others in a long line at the post office or even at the coffee shop you go to every workday. The question is: Are you making the most of your time and the opportunities available to you each and every day?

ACTION:

Over the course of the next week, take note of how many *new* people you encounter. And yes, seatmates on the bus count!

Chapter 1

What Is a Networking Event?

Let's First Define Networking

Before we dig into what a networking event is, let's start with the definition of the word network. According to *The Oxford Dictionary*:

nétwerk n. & v. a group of people who exchange information, contacts, and experience for professional or social purposes.

Therefore, networking can be defined as one's efforts to create this group.

And, in that same vein, a 2009 study on professional networking and career advancement, sponsored by Upwardly Mobile, Inc. (http://www.upmo.com) and Pepperdine's Graziadio School of Business Management (http://bschool.pepperdine.edu), defined networking as:

Proactively reaching out to colleagues, finding answers to colleague questions, researching future connections and making new connections.

Does networking mean you're looking to use people to achieve selfish goals, or opportunistically ask people for help? No, of course not! In fact, almost all your networking can help other people as much as it can help you. In any industry or career level, networking helps you make connections in a personal way. It aids you in building relationships of support and respect, and enables you to discover and create mutually beneficial connections.

How can you ensure this? For starters, next time you set out to "network," instead of thinking "What can I get out of this?" think, "What can I give to this?" It's an approach no serious professional in any field or at any career stage should go without today. In fact, early in their careers, folks in the sales and marketing arenas learn that you never know where you might meet your next key contact, partner, client, or even new friend. But remember, building relationships takes time and the best networking starts when you don't need it. Then when you do need it, those connections are available.

While events focused solely on networking are everywhere these days, most of us have also noticed that conferences and other professional gatherings often carve out specific networking sections to their programming. It might be before the sessions begin for the day or after a day's worth of training seminars, during a happy hour. And then in some cases, industry networking events are instead called "socials," and sometimes they go by the term "open house."

Today, thanks to many of the online social networking tools created within the past 10 years, it's pretty obvious that networking matters to just about everyone.

Why Do People Bother Networking?

Another way to think about networking is as the deliberate process of making connections for mutual benefit. However, whether you network to make friends (new to town), find a new job, source candidates, develop your current career, explore new career options, learn, conduct research, obtain referrals, collect intel, or simply to broaden your professional horizons, it is important to focus on networking as an exchange of information, contacts, or experiences.

There's also the fact that unless you love cold calling, networking is one of the most effective ways to generate leads and referrals for whatever it is you're looking. For lots of professionals today, many of the people attending in-person events or participating in an online discussion could be potential employees, clients, employers, or even vendors, as well as referral sources for any of these things.

According to an April 2009 study by AfterCollege®, *the most effective job search method by the 4.4% who had an easy time finding work* (26 out of 670 respondents) was something you can only do via personal networking:

Seventy-six percent said speaking to someone who already works at the company of interest was **the** way to do it.

The study also pointed out that while social networking sites were used heavily by many of the respondents, their effectiveness in finding a job was reflected in only 11% of the responses. And compared to the above, only 4% of those who found their job search easy, mentioned social networks as being effective tools.

Job search methods found effective by those who had an easy time finding work		
Speak to someone who already works at the company of interest	76%	19
Apply directly to the company/organization	72%	18
Search an online job board (e.g. AfterCollege, Monster, CareerBuilder)	68%	17
Speak to a professor, teacher, instructor, or dean	64%	16
Speak to friends and/or family members	60%	15
Attend a school career fair	56%	14
Visit the career section of the organization/corporation's site	56%	14
Contact an employment contractor, agency, or recruiter	44%	11
Attend on-campus information sessions/interviews	40%	10
Visit the career center at your school	36%	9
Network at an association or club (trade/industry)	36%	9
Look in the newspaper	32%	8
Read/subscribe to an e-newsletter	16%	4
Read about it or chat about it in a blog that pertained to a career interest	12%	3
Chat about it at a social networking site, such as Facebook or LinkedIn	4%	1

A survey recommendation:

Network through personal touch, and don't rely on social networking.

Use emerging technologies to enhance your existing personal networking, but don't let technology replace those activities. Speaking to someone who works at a company of interest was rated as one of the most effective ways of finding a job.

(Source: AfterCollege® Student & Alumni Snapshot Survey, AfterCollege, Inc. April 2009)

The 2009 study published by Upwardly Mobile, Inc. (http://www.upmo.com) offered some additional insights and even identified an enviable group they call the networking "elite." Despite the plethora of online tools out there, this group of high-earning and high career-level professionals still manages to achieve truly effective networking by whacking through the weeds and focusing on what matters—real, mutually beneficial partnerships.

They found that the "elites" identified in their study have learned by experience how to leverage networking to serve others, create rapport, proactively manage relationships, channel the right information and opportunities, and accelerate their journeys along chosen career paths. Elites have clearly learned to leverage today's online networking paradigm to break barriers of gender, education, age, class and proximity.

The study cites:

Elites know what most "networking" professionals do not: that effective networking today is about quickly cutting through the clutter and creating meaningful online and offline connections, relationships and rapport—the kind that enable the giving and receiving of trust. Elites also know that anyone, at any salary level, can "do" effective networking; our study shows that networking is a key driver behind higher salaries and career advancement.

Elite networkers report networking as enabling access to pre-qualified resources that give them "an edge." In their own words:

"Networking is a great way to access a pre-qualified talent pool; it's like I already had the initial interview."
– Elite Networker

"I network for publicity; I blog and write, too. I want people to know who I am. Networking is, most importantly, about access to resources. I noticed other execs always had a virtual team they could call on. They always found the right resource, and it gave them an edge.... Adding people to your network is like building a friendship: you have to dedicate some time and effort to it."
– Elite Networker, CFO, Startup

"I network to stay connected to the business community and identify potential work. Business development is constant for me, and I found that the best way to develop new business is through referrals. Another reason is to maintain an awareness of what's going on in the industry. Yet another is to stay connected with colleagues."
– Elite Networker, VP

"Give away your time, talent, effort and treasure, and you will gain something else."
– Elite Networker, SVP

(Source: Professional Networking and Career Advancement Report, Upwardly Mobile, Inc. 2009)

2 How Do You Prepare for a Networking Event?

Doing the best at this moment puts you in the best place for the next moment.
– **Oprah Winfrey**

Do Some Research and Then Come Up With a Plan

As you'll glean as I continue, I'm a huge fan of LinkedIn and log in to my currently upgraded (Professional version) account daily, and sometimes, more than twice a day. I recommend that you use LinkedIn (or other online search methods if you can't find what you're looking for in LinkedIn) to check out the hosts, speakers, or sponsors of events. And if the invite or attendee list is accessible, definitely give it a scan to see if you know anyone that might also be attending, or if anyone you've been hoping to meet will be there. Today, many event hosts are creating LinkedIn or Facebook groups so you can check out the profiles of the folks who have joined those groups and are attending the event. Perhaps even look up the speaker's or presenter's name in LinkedIn and see if anyone you know is connected to them. It's always a great networking tactic to introduce yourself to the speaker or host, and if you enjoyed their presentation to tell them so and/or to introduce yourself and mention your mutual connection, if you have identified one. Oftentimes speakers appear at an event solo and welcome a friendly face belonging to a person with whom they share a mutual connection.

In support of learning to love LinkedIn, a January 2009 study of 583 IT pros by Network World cited that the number one social networking site they used was LinkedIn, with 63% of respondents having used it, while Facebook usage came in at 44%. (The last time they conducted the study—in December 2007—it showed that only 41% had used LinkedIn, while Facebook was at only 20%.)

Once You're There

There's already been so much written about how to get started when faced with a roomful of strangers or work a room, so I'm not going to spend too much time on this, because you must go with what is comfortable for you. Maybe you prefer to approach a small group with a smile and a nod, or perhaps approaching a lone wallflower is more your speed because you can then no longer be wallflowers together. Be sure to mingle though, and try not to stay in one area all night, talking to the same group of people. Remember, the general idea is to meet and introduce yourself to as many people as you are comfortable with, so make it one of your goals to circulate. Whatever your preference, how you introduce yourself will make an impact on the people you meet and will likely help determine whether or not they actually remember you and/or your company. Practice your introduction whenever you can (yes, you need to!) and focus on being memorable.

Come up with something clever, like an Accounts Receivable manager I know did. It goes something like this:

"Hi! I'm Samantha Kent and I'm a money wrangler at Acme Enterprises." People often then try to guess what she does (if she's not at a CPA event), and they fairly often think she's in investment banking or, these days, maybe someone working in bank auditing. A recent grad, new to the job market, might say, "Hi, I'm Ben Zabel and I'm a newly-minted CPA aspiring to someday run the US Mint." A little humor goes a long way in most industries, so a tongue-in-cheek opener like this will not only make you memorable, it will also help create conversation, which usually makes things more relaxed. It needs to be clever though, so ask a friend for help or poll your contacts via an online group in which you participate.

Depending on what your goals are, I'm a big believer in crafting your intro as something between what some call a "bumper sticker" (a.k.a. personal tagline) and an elevator speech (a.k.a. pitch). Depending on the circumstances, you might need the former more than the latter, so start thinking of one for yourself. I sometime use:

"I'm Sandy Jones-Kaminski and I'm a strategic business developer and social capital expert. I have my own consulting business called Bella Domain and if I had a bumper sticker made for my business it would say "Connecting You to Relationships That Matter.""

If the situation calls for a somewhat lengthier elevator speech (by the way, apparently the length of the average elevator ride can be anywhere from 30 to about 60 seconds), just be sure it is clear and concise. It must quickly explain what you do and how you add value.

Here's an example:

"My name is Sandy Jones-Kaminski and I am a business development and partnership marketing strategist. I specialize in helping early stage executives generate more opportunities, create new revenue streams and close more deals. My approach is data driven and based on my 15+ years of market development and account management work. That experience, when combined with my background in market research, operations and connecting, makes me uniquely qualified to work with Inc 1000 executives in an effective and highly productive way. Basically, I help them develop strategic relationships and create new opportunities."

I asked Sima Dahl, President of Parlay Communications, Ltd., Founder of the Marketing Job Wire, in Chicago, and author of the forthcoming book titled, 'Sway Factor: The Art of Networking in a Digital Age,' to give me her tips on crafting an elevator pitch:

Sima suggests that a good elevator pitch is:

- **Short:** You've got 30 seconds or about 100 words to make your point.

- **Simple:** Focus on a singular, high-level concept; you can fill in the details later.

- **Intriguing:** Why is it unique? Come up with a hook. "I own a laundromat downtown" doesn't hold a candle to "I run the only eco-friendly laundromat in Chicago and cater to green-minded urban professionals."

- **Exciting:** Why are you excited to get up each morning and go to work on this idea? Being exciting helps you be memorable.

- **Well-rehearsed:** It should roll off your tongue with ease and with passion.

Take a minute to consider your pitch. If it needs tuning, answer these three questions:

1. Who are you?
2. What business are you in?
3. Why is it special?

Know How to Ask for What You Need

You then want to think about making it easy for the other person to help you by articulating what it is that you're looking for right now. Being clear about what defines an ideal opportunity for you, makes everyone's life easier. Here are a few examples:

"I'm a start-up junkie and love their fast-paced cultures, so right now I'm seeking to identify and connect with senior staffers or founders who are involved in a startup venture of some kind, as well as any service provider such as angel investors, VC firms, private equity advisors, attorneys, or outsourced HR firms who might support these folks closely and know what's going on around town in terms of new companies getting funded or launched."

"A good prospect for me is a chief executive, president or vice president of business development at any early-stage company that needs a hand with strategic growth and has a team of at least 10 or more in place."

"I'm looking to make a change and I saw an opening over at Bella Domain Design recently that really interests me; do you happen to know anybody at that firm who might be able to help me get a foot in the door?"

"I've spent the past week researching 10 companies I know are hiring right now where I think my skills and experience would be put to good use; would you mind reviewing my list for me and letting me know if you've heard anything about hiring or new product launches at any of these firms?"

"I just launched a blog about the Denver Organic dining scene and am looking for wanna-be foodies to read it, share recommendations, and help spread the word. It's called 'Organic Denver Style' and my last post was about the new Alice Waters restaurant."

Plan to Keep It Casual

Of course, it's always best to strive to develop a casual conversation at first. A networking function is an ideal way to have people get to know you. In business, as well as in personal dealings, it is in everyone's best interest to make an effort to try to create a relaxed and personal environment in which to introduce yourself or your company. Referencing your standard cocktail party or wedding guest, small talk will help you come up with a few easy conversation starters. Try openers like, "So, Bob, how are you connected to this group/the host(s)?" or, "What brought you to this particular event out of the many going on in town?" You can even use an old standby just like the Obamas did when they had to dance with numerous complete strangers during the many Inaugural balls, and ask "So, where are you from Master Sergeant Davis?"

ACTION:

Develop your own list of openers along the lines of those above or these:

- How has the economy been affecting you or your business this year?

- Are you originally from the Bay Area?

- What did you think the speaker's best take away was today?

Pay attention to the answers to these questions so that you can master Chapter 6, and because being able to follow up with the people you meet, by sending them a relevant article or idea as a result of what you discovered while talking to them, is one of the best ways to cultivate your new connection.

Be Sure You Visually Stand Out, But in a "Good" Way

Believe it or not, another smart way to be memorable, as well as productive at an event, is to wear something in a bright color or that is unique, such as a printed or patterned shirt. Most folks will have an easier time pointing you out to others during the event and then also remembering you when you follow up with them later on. My follow-up emails often include, "Hi Ben, I was the gal wearing the red scarf and jacket in that group of four we were part of Tuesday morning."

What You Should Wear to Professional and Casual Networking Events

Sometimes networking events can be trickier to dress for than a normal day at the office, because, like it or not, what you wear often has an impact on how people perceive you. And since most people form an impression of you before you even offer them a smile or hand to shake, projecting the image you want is important in order to create the right impression.

Today, most people should wear business casual to the majority of the networking events they attend. What's business casual? It's basically a more relaxed version of what used to be referred to as conservative "office attire." It does not mean you're actually going to be "casual" per se. In most cases, it is likely going to be your usual office dress code if you work in a semi-conservative workplace. For women, business casual is a shirt with a collar and/or a sweater, khakis or dress pants and nice shoes. Women may also sometimes wear a moderate length dress or skirt. For men, business casual might be a polo shirt or shirt with a collar and/or sweater, khakis or dress pants and dress shoes, but no tie is required.

The only exception might be if there's a stated dress code (i.e., black tie because the event is a fund raiser) or you're coming from a very conservative office environment, so you simply wear what you wore to work that day. And, depending on where you live in the U.S., you can also expect to see people dressed slightly more **trendy (or fashion forward)** than you would in a typical office.

Practice Your Small Talk

Most importantly, get comfortable with small talk, if you aren't already. Practice everywhere you can. This includes places like the grocery store, the drive-up window, on an airplane, or at a lunch counter. Think about setting a goal to speak to at least one stranger every day, and, no, glib comments on Facebook do not count. You can choose to initiate, but even something as simple as "I'm fine, thanks, and how about you?" counts as a conversation-starting response.

ACTION:

Talk to at least one stranger each day and try initiating with a "How's your day going?"

Do Your Research and Always Have a Goal

You can also strive to make in-person networking less stressful, more productive, and even enjoyable by setting goals. Having a mission or goal will help create focus, which usually helps relieve nervousness. Whatever you do, keep your expectations reasonable and don't let your valuable time and energy at in-person networking events be wasted.

Good goals to set include:

- Meeting specific people

- Qualifying prospective employees or hiring managers

- Collecting certain information

- Developing current or new business relationships, as well as mutually supportive friendships

Let's say you have the need for a referral into the hot new game development company in town and you know they are currently hiring, and it's for something perfectly suited for you like a game producer. As you mentally prepare for the event, be sure to set a goal for yourself that you'll share your plans for a change in your employment status with at least two people. You can then encourage the folks you meet to give you a heads up should they learn that

   a. they either have a connection that can potentially help you or,
   b. if they soon meet someone who can.

Also, remember, one of the advantages of in-person networking events is that once you tell one person you meet what you're looking for, if you've made a good impression, they'll likely suggest other people find you as they work their way around the event. (Here's where having worn a polka-dot blouse comes into play.) Folks often do this when they hear someone new to them speak of something related to you or your recently shared goal.

ACTION:

Plan how you'll share your goals with at least 3 other attendees.

WARNING: It IS a little scary and kind of tough out there right now!

Partly thanks to all the online social networking tools available (which I do love), we have an over abundance of people who think that the odd and misplaced, often snarky, quip (think Facebook status update comments or direct Tweets here), or name dropping in order to "friend" someone, or stalking (I saw you were at the Sounders game last night, and I was wondering where you got that sweet Battlestar Galactica t-shirt you had on?), and then the posturing "I'm a social media expert," are all ways you meet up with someone in person. Well, not so much.

But, tell me, is any of that working for you? And how do you measure your success? As I said, I love all the social networking tools available, and spend way more time on them than I probably should, but I don't measure my success by the number of friends or followers I have, and I'll match the power of my quality-based network over someone's quantity-based one any day. Don't get me wrong, it's nice to have "friends," but what you really need are **real** connections to help make things happen. What's a "real connection?" It's one where when you ask them for a favor they say, "Yes, of course." and then they actually do it, or if they can't, they offer another option or at least manage to be helpful.

On this topic, the Professional Networking and Career Advancement Report mentioned previously also noted that:

"Despite the current trend among established professional networking tools and sites to acknowledge and honor users based on network size, professionals do not feel size is what brings value to networks. By 33 percentage points, *depth of personal relationship* trumped *number of overall contacts/connections*. Relationship depth also scored significantly higher—by 20 percentage points—than the willingness of a contact to recommend."

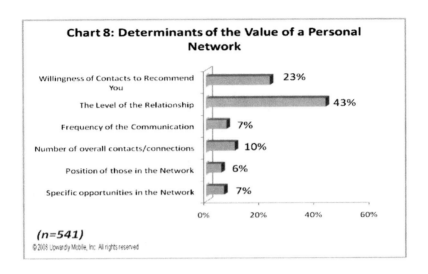

(Source: Professional Networking and Career Advancement Report, Upwardly Mobile, Inc. 2009)

3 Where Do Networking Events Take Place?

Enjoy yourself. If you can't enjoy yourself, enjoy someone else.
– **Jack Schaefer**

Personally, I find that networking opportunities exist everywhere I go. Of course, there are the obvious places like conferences, professional association luncheons, seminars, forums, Bunko nights, wedding receptions, class reunions, cocktail parties, and so on. I have even met people in the line at the post office, after "dropping eaves" on a discussion about favorite parts of Italy to explore. Thanks to my sharing that I too loved the Cinque Terre, I ended up making a new friend to dine out with at all the trendy Italian restaurants that had opened just prior to my moving back to Chicago. This type of networking, and lots of other situations like it, helped me rebuild my network there, after being away for over 4 years. Cindy and I are still in touch today—thank you, Facebook!

The People That You Will Meet

Some of the event attendees might be people with goals similar to yours, or perhaps even diametrically opposed to yours, i.e., they want the same game developer job or similar prospects for their promotional products business. I believe that at some point (and usually early on) we each decide if we're going to be a collaborative type of person or the competitive type. Both have a place in this world, and in certain scenarios, one might be more advantageous than the other, but I'd argue that this only holds true for indiscriminate periods of time. Sooner of later, you will find yourself needing to wear the other hat or wishing someone else was wearing it. Keep this in mind as you encounter others.

My personal philosophy is that it is always best to seek common ground first, then respectfully acknowledge whether or where there might be a conflict, and either politely move on or classify the situation as a "collabortition" (collaboration + competition) and keep it friendly. Wouldn't it be incredible though, if we cultivated an environment where competition to be first and collaboration and sharing of knowledge are the norm? Something that inspires this idea is a sentence my friend, Aaron Fairchild, often writes in his follow-up emails, "I am a true believer in collaboration and the notion that a rising tide lifts all boats."

There's Always a Host

Let's also recognize that at most networking events there is always someone acting in the role of a host (even if the bar is no-host), and one of your goals should be to seek out that person or a rep from the host entity to thank them and introduce yourself. It could be a board president or member, or a VP of Marketing, or a city council member, or even a small business owner. Think of it as you would a party you've been invited to in someone's home, and show graciousness by saying hello and thanking them for hosting. If you've never ever hosted anything (not even a backyard BBQ or a dorm room party), and can't relate to this, then it might be time to start thinking about hosting your own event, and be sure to read the bonus chapter at the end of this book titled "How to Have Your Own Networking Event."

But let's assume you've done this, and they've smiled back and shook your hand. You should feel free to use this moment to do at least one of the 2 things:

1. Tell them you were excited to come to the event because you were hoping to meet someone from Halocraft Studios, and did they by any chance know if they've arrived, and if they know them, would they be willing to introduce you.

2. Take the pay it forward stance, and mention that you're a social media enthusiast and ask if they know anyone that might want to "pick my brain" about setting up a Facebook or LinkedIn group.

Most hosts or sponsors want their events to be a success, and one of the ways to do this is by making introductions and facilitating in such a way that the goals of their attendees and guests are met.

When Networking Online...

When networking with new or professionally related connections online, you **really** need to pay attention to the impact that tone can have in your digital communications. It's important that you watch the cheekiness in your messaging, and wait until you have first established a personal rapport with people. What a shame it would be to turn off a potentially great new relationship, by losing them over a snarky comment in an email or in response to their Status Update. Also, please be brief! Too many people think the online channel is a replace-ment to the letters or memos of old. It is not! Today, most people don't even read their messages on a monitor. Instead, they read them hurriedly on a tiny little screen. Long messages tend to get saved with the intention that they'll be read more thoroughly later, but usually end up forgotten because they've become buried in an inbox, or, even worse, saved in a rarely opened folder.

Chapter 3: Where Do Networking Events Take Place?

4 What Do You Need to Do Once You Are There?

The more you try to be interested in other people, the more you find out about yourself.
– Thea Astley

Check Yourself

First things first...hit the bathroom and check your appearance when you arrive at a networking event. Make sure you look good (or at least not frazzled or weather beaten) and that you don't have something left over from your last meal stuck in your teeth. Remember, there's nothing like making a good first impression, so be sure to smile! Smiling is something that is easy to forget (especially if you're a little nervous), but it is so important to do. The callout center staff I used to oversee in Chicago had reminder signs in their cubicles that said "Smile While You Dial," because if you smile while you're on the phone the entire tone of your voice changes; so can you imagine what happens if you wear a smile in person?

Almost as important as how you look, is how you act. Your general attitude says so much about you when you first meet people, so make sure you're focused on exuding some positive energy.

Be sure you keep your body language open by standing up straight and keeping your arms at your sides and your shoulders back. Folding your arms makes you look closed off, which is the exact opposite of what you're going for at a networking event. If you're nervous, imagine that you're walking into a room full of all your closet friends and try to relax.

Be Present and Mindful

In the fast-paced world we live in, we've grown accustomed to juggling three or four tasks at once, and often don't give our full attention to the task at hand. While we can often get away with this in our own little worlds, and can fix any mishaps that occur, when we're engaging with other people we need to be fully present. I can't tell you how many eyes I see darting around at events while the person who those eyes belong to is either talking or supposedly listening to another person. I recognize that this may be due to ADHD or some illness like it—but come on people, please don't do that!

It's also not an online environment where you might try to be the first person to blurt out some clever quip while someone is still speaking, and come to think of it, even in those environments, don't you have to wait for them to finish before you can comment? It's no different in person. Learn to be an active listener, or as I've started asking people, "Please stop being a poster child for the hard of listening!"

My advice is to try using something called "mindfulness" to be fully present. This simply involves being attentive to the moment, listening intently, and slowing down just a tad to be in the present or the "now." Mindfulness may sound like something new age, but the ideas behind it are centuries old. The key is to be fully present in the moment, without judgment, but with focus. Without focus on the present moment, you are less likely to succeed at whatever you are doing, especially listening. Many people find that when they set the intention to be an active listener they become more attentive and alert and can even maintain calmness of mind. Did you know that Tiger Woods attributes much of his success to his practice of mindfulness?

And if that's not enough to convince you to give it a try, consider this, in Guy Kawasaki's latest book called 'Reality Check,' he says, "The mark of a good conversationalist is not that you can talk a lot. The mark is that you can get others to talk a lot...."

ACTION:

Before heading out to your next networking event, practice being an active listener with a friendly stranger by giving these a try:

1. receive information from others while remaining non-judgmental and empathic,

2. acknowledge the speaker in a way that invites the communication to continue, and

3. provide a limited but encouraging response, carrying the speaker's idea one step forward.

Offer Help to Others First

While you're hopefully prepared and clear on your goals, a lot of other folks coming to events have done the same prep work, so think about being the first to ask others what brought them to the event or what it is they need help with right now. We all usually have something that we could use an assist on, don't we?

So, go to an event with the intention to help. Just ask a question like, "So, Bob, do you need help with anything in your world right now?" Or, perhaps while you are listening to Bob's intro or elevator speech, a person you know pops into your mind (your brother-in-law maybe), who you realize could be a good resource for Bob to connect with regarding the best associations to join for electrical engineers. Well, don't hesitate to offer to connect Bob to them and simply consider it an easy "pay it forward" in the karma bank. Because when you're least expecting it, you'll soon likely be the recipient of some good karma of your own.

Call it the "give to get" or Potlatch style (Native American reference), Networlding, NetWeaving—it's all the same and all of it is good.

Remember, when you go to a networking event and are *solely* focused on getting your own needs met, it is true that most people you meet will "smell" the greed or desperation coming from you. Instead, focus on how you can help other people, and by offering your help, others are more likely to give you theirs. For example, at a social or business function you may spot the opportunity to suggest an online resource for a problem someone is trying to solve, answer a technical question, introduce a person to someone else who may be of interest, promise to send a link to an article on the subject you discussed, or simply go up to talk to someone standing alone. These are all great ways to offer help.

Most of my reluctant networker clients report that when they attend events with the goal of helping, they feel more at ease. Some report, with some surprise, that they actually kind of enjoy themselves if they take this approach.

NOTE: If one of your goals is to meet as many sources of referrals as possible at an event, it's best to keep track of time, and try not to spend more than ten minutes or so with each person and continue to mingle.

As you meet people you think you can help or would like to form a connection with, exchange contact info so you can follow up to set appointments to get together with anyone who seems promising. You can easily say, "Bob, I'll send you my brother-in-law's contact info if you give me your card, and here's mine. And I'd love to take you up on your offer to share your advice on the best way to present an opportunity to your former employer. May I contact you to set up a call or coffee date for next week?" At your next meeting you can then take additional time to discover how you could possibly continue to help each other.

More On Offering Help to Others First

These reprints of two blog posts are written by a quality connection of mine, named Matt Youngquist. Matt is a Seattle-based executive career coach and outplacement consultant at Career Horizons (http://www.career-horizons.com). Matt authors a great blog in general, but these particular posts were worth including because he is writing specifically about the "give to get" concept. He has coached hundreds of people on their job search strategies, and in my opinion, Matt really knows his stuff:

Give to Get: The Potlatch Principle (May 26, 2009)

Given the avalanche of books, literature, and blog articles that have been produced on the subject of "networking" over the past decade, it can be tough to find something new to contribute to the discussion, at times! By now, most professionals (especially those in transition) have heard the same key networking themes dogmatically repeated dozens, if not hundreds, of times during their search:

1. *60–80% of all jobs come through the "hidden" job market of networking and personal contacts;*
2. *Social networking websites (e.g. Facebook, Biznik, LinkedIn) are now indispensable tools in the networking arsenal; and*
3. *Your networking shouldn't be 100% one-sided; you should practice a "give to get" philosophy for best results*

It's around the third point above, however, that I wanted to add a few thoughts that I haven't seen talked about much in the networking literature to date. As an avid fan of history, and sociology, I'm always on the lookout (to a fault, probably) for connections between supposedly "new" job hunting principles and other aspects of civilization that have been around for hundreds or thousands of years. To me, finding these connections is not just fun, but helps me get a better grasp on why certain principles work, how long they've worked, and how best to explain them to other people who may not be as familiar with them on a day-to-day basis.

So on that note, let's talk for a second about the idea that we can all get more of what we want out of life by focusing on giving things to others, versus getting things ourselves. Frankly, I think most of us would agree that this notion makes sense. Nobody likes being used, after all, and I'm sure all of us have had the experience of having been asked for a big favor by somebody who then disappears without a word of thanks, a thoughtful follow-up note, or a single gesture of reciprocity. When this happens, too, I'm sure we all tend to kick ourselves and promise that we'll never lift a finger to help the ingrate in question again, right? I mean, I don't know about you, but I certainly have a "mental blacklist" (thankfully a very short one!) of people from the past to whom I gave, and gave, and gave, and didn't ever really seem to "get back" from. So to avoid becoming one of these people, myself, I consciously focus on trying to help other people and reciprocate as much as possible, knowing that these efforts are mostly likely to keep the door open for future favors.

As for the origins of this whole two-way networking notion, one could certainly argue that Dale Carnegie was the first person who brought the "give to get" concept to the masses in his 1936 classic "How to Win Friends and Influence People." Since then, numerous authors have slapped their own spin on the same concept and re-branded it. For example, there are variations on the theme found in both Norman Vincent Peale's 'The Power of Positive Thinking' as well as Stephen Covey's '7 Habits of Highly Effective People' books. You'll also find a metaphysical twist on the principle running throughout all of the "Law of Attraction" titles that have come out in recent years. Every few decades, like clockwork, somebody seems to resuscitate this pearl of interpersonal wisdom, package it for the next generation, and sell a few million dollars' worth of books and self-help videos.

My belief, however, is that there's a community out there that's got even Mr. Carnegie beat in terms of espousing the "give to get" concept in an organized way. Who might that be? Growing up in Juneau, Alaska, we spent a fair amount of time in school studying the history of the local Native tribes, and I remember being taught that these communities routinely held a special type of party called a "potlatch" where the hosts would (among other rites) make a point of giving away lavish gifts to all of their guests, almost to the point of impoverishment. The more valuable the gifts given, the greater the esteem and respect would be accorded to the hosts. To cite the relevant Wikipedia entry on the subject, in a Potlatch culture "the status of any given family is raised not by who has the most resources, but by who distributes the most resources."

So when it comes to the idea that giving freely to other people is the best route to achieving success, both among one's network and among the community at large, I think the Pacific Northwest tribes get the prize for fleshing this idea out first in formalized fashion. In fact, I'll confess that whenever I hear the "give to get" guideline cited by various networking experts out there, I automatically translate the concept into "The Potlatch Principle" in my head, since this label helps me both understand it, as well as remember and practice it in my own business ventures.

Pretty esoteric stuff, I realize, and I wouldn't be surprised a bit if some of you immediately start forwarding me some literature proving that the ancient Greeks, Egyptians, or some other ancient civilization was routinely preaching/practicing the two-way networking shtick even earlier! As I mentioned, though, it's hard to find anything terribly original to add to the sea of networking advice out there, so I thought I'd dust off my keyboard today and give it my best shot.

Give to Get: Game Theory (May 26, 2009)

Ready for esoteric networking commentary, part two?

While composing my previous article, about the tie-in between the famous "give to get" networking principle and the "potlatch" rite practiced by a number of Native American tribes in the Pacific Northwest, it struck me that there was one other geeky example I could share where modern job search advice seems to intersect with the annals of art, science, and history. Again, folks, I realize it's a sickness, so forgive me. But I just love it when I spot a new twist or juicy, corroborating case study about networking that I haven't seen anybody talk about before out there....

So this time around, we're going to talk about the fascinating world of game theory. If you really want to know more about this field, click here,[2] but the cliff-notes version is that it involves scientists and mathematicians applying complex formulas, algorithms, and simulations to try to uncover the keys to successful strategy—be it of the military, corporate, board game, or "winning in life" variety. And in these studies, if you peer closely enough, you'll find empirical echoes of the "give to get" networking philosophy playing out, as well.

---

2. http://en.wikipedia.org/wiki/Game_theory

One famous experiment, for example, demonstrated that the most successful and stable long-term strategy for individuals living within a community was to **always cooperate with the people around them as the first option.** *To quote a few relevant passages about this study, again from Wikipedia: "Greedy strategies tended to do very poorly in the long run while more altruistic strategies did better, as judged purely by self-interest." Additionally, after conducting the experiment, Robert Axelrod [game theory expert and professor of Political Science & Public Policy at the University of Michigan] reached "the oxymoronic-sounding conclusion that selfish individuals for their own selfish good will tend to be nice and forgiving and non-envious."*

How accurate or controlled was this particular experiment? I can't say for sure, since I can barely remember how to do long division, much less understand the level of math involved in this kind of thing. But setting that issue aside for a moment, if you re-read the paragraph above, there's one part that really caught my attention and that relates back to the key point of this article, which is how these concepts relate to business and career networking. If you read the quote again, you'll notice that the experiments in question weren't examining the benefits of cooperation from an ethical standpoint or for the sake of community welfare as a whole. They were testing the effectiveness of cooperation (i.e. reciprocity) solely as a **self-interested strategy designed to help the individual in question "win" and satisfy their OWN personal wants and needs***.*

This, to me, is the really intriguing part. According to these experiments, even if one truly does view networking solely as a means to an end, from a purely self-interested "how can I leverage the people around me to get help/leads/referrals?" point of view, these studies still suggest that the key to success is to practice a help-others-first strategy as opposed to just going out and strip-mining your Rolodex for favors. Scientifically proven? Absolutely beyond dispute? Directly relevant to your own daily networking efforts? I'll leave those questions up to you to answer, but I thought it was some interesting food for thought, at the very least...

Keep It Consistent

In today's social networking climate, you should have already established an online reputation/brand, and according to some experts, if you can't be personally goggled, you might not as well exist. Also, be sure to keep your in-person, or offline professional brand, consistent with your online "professional" personal brand (how you identify yourself). For most folks, we're talking about what you share on LinkedIn or BizNik™ here. One of the worst disconnects to have is the values and personal brand projected on one channel radically different from another. Most professionals can definitely benefit from reading Guy Kawasaki's blog post (http://blog.guykawasaki.com/2007/01/linkedin_profil.html) about tweaking your profile on LinkedIn. Today, most online profiles need to read almost exactly as you do in person. This is a good thing. Who wants to come across in bullet point form or sound like their resume or CV?

And now for a few words about and from my favorite business networking tool, LinkedIn. As the mother of all business networking sites states:

Your professional network of trusted contacts gives you an advantage in your career, and is one of your most valuable assets. LinkedIn exists to help you make better use of your professional network and help the people you trust in return.

Our mission is to connect the world's professionals to accelerate their success. We believe that in a global connected economy, your success as a professional and your competitiveness as a company depends upon faster access to insight and resources you can trust.

LinkedIn is an interconnected network of experienced professionals from around the world, representing 170 industries and 200 countries. You can find, be introduced to, and collaborate with qualified professionals that you need to work with to accomplish your goals.

I'm a huge fan of online social and business networking tools like LinkedIn, but that's all they are—tools. And, yes, social networking sites can be a very powerful tools for communicating with people, but you still have to know how to genuinely connect with them, and be adept at occasionally interacting in person, over coffee or perhaps at a networking event.

And, whatever you do, try not to get a reputation as an abuser of LinkedIn. Some overly aggressive linkers are part of a controversial group within LinkedIn, called "promiscuous linkers." It's a reputation that is hard to shake once you get it, and regardless whether you *are* a recruiter, or intend to use your networks to market and promote yourself or your products, or services, or jobs, my advice is to tread very carefully here. As the article below mentions, "LinkedIn has tried to discourage "link banking" by showing a maximum of 500 connections on a profile page, but that has done little to stop the practice." Once again, quality over quantity is usually the best way to go. If you're still not sure just what exactly a promiscuous linker is, then read this still-relevant article from the former Business 2.0 Magazine titled, "The Missing Link." http://tinyurl.com/yztbvu

I asked my friend, the savvy marketer and conscientious networker, Geoff Tucker (http://blog.geofftucker.com) what advice he wanted to share regarding the many things he has learned about using LinkedIn effectively, and he offered the following insights and suggestions:

- Modify the title to be *you*—not a job title (for example, "Marketing Communications Manager" not "MarCom Specialist Level II").

- It is good to post your picture when trying to bypass HR to reach the hiring manager. This puts a face with a name, and offers an opportunity to let the hiring manager identify with you. ("He looks like a nice guy, someone I'd enjoy talking to.")

- Modify the profile URL to have your name in it. If your name is already taken, add your middle initial or middle name. When a person searches for you on LinkedIn, the geographical constraints will reduce the search results enough to make you easy to find. When googled (and you will be), your profile will now appear in Google search results.

- Privacy settings: Turn these to "no" when making major updates. Leaving it to "yes" means every time you change even one letter in a word, your contacts are notified that your profile has been updated—but it doesn't say what you did. Make all your updates in one session, and then turn privacy back to "yes" so people will see only your fully revised profile. You don't want to fatigue your contacts with excessive updates about you that aren't really updates.

- Be a lifetime learner, always reading, always learning. Be a trendspotter. Focus on employability, not job titles. The days of lifetime employment are dead and mostly a myth of the manufacturing economy. Your career is yours to manage and own. Focus on bringing value to your role, not just skills.

- Profile Summary: Do not write this as dry as a resume is. Give the reader more to read. If you are in a creative profession, be creative because you are expected to be. This is the time and place to demonstrate your character and qualities. Show personality, show enthusiasm, and make yourself stand out from cookie-cutter profiles.

- Read other people's profiles for ideas of what to write about yourself. If writing isn't your strong suit, imitation is the highest form of flattery. Read profiles of people in your field, at your level, and find the ones who say it well. Then copy, put your own spin on it, and paste.

- Be authentically you in what you say. If the words you say feel fake to you, imagine how they will sound to the person reading it.

- I love this metaphor: "Social networks are how we have a front porch since we are now so transient." Using online social networks are how we keep up with everyone. This is called "ambient awareness" by social media experts.

- Your resume is a reason to get someone to call you. When they ask about your experiences, don't tell them **how** you did it. Tell them what you did and the results. Tease them. Make them want more. If you tell them the *how*, you solved their problem (by giving them the answer), and now they can do it on their own. And you got bupkus for it.

- Understand your market and your audience so you can talk to them how they expect you to. If talking to marketers, use a marketer's language. If talking to a recruiter, use language that she can follow. Remember: a recruiter fills many positions, so they don't necessarily know every industry's jargon.

- Get Recommendations! Reciprocate always. Talk about the person's work, talk about him as a person. Pay it forward.

- Connect with LinkedIn Open Networkers (LIONs) to generate many 3rd degree connections. You may never meet the LION, but the 3rd degree connection opens up pathways to many more people. LIONs are good to move your message forward when requested. Again, pay it forward and reciprocate.

- Write a recommendation even if you only know a little bit about the person. Speak to the qualities you have seen and experienced.

- Searching technique:

    - Use Boolean searches. Put search terms in double quotes to constrain search results. Modify by using AND, OR and NOT (in all caps) between search terms. For example, "John Doe" AND Starbucks.

- Join Groups. Similar to connecting with LIONs, having a group in common lets you easily connect with others on your own. Also, groups are a great way to network online and in person. They range from your location, to your industry, to diversity groups and more.

- Search for points of affinity when searching for people. For example, search for people from your university alma mater, from companies where you worked, or by job titles. If you want to connect with accounting supervisors in your city, search by job titles in your area to find them. Then use 3rd degree connections through groups or LIONs to network with them.

Chapter

5 What Should You *Not* Do At a Networking Event?

You can make more friends in two months by becoming interested in other people than you can in two years by trying to get other people interested in you.
– Dale Carnegie

Don't Be a Business Card Commando

If you are a compulsive business card collector, please stop it. Handing out your business card to 50 people you talked to for about thirty seconds each, not only makes you look self-serving and desperate, it also sends off a clear message that you're most likely going to spam people with your newsletter, resume or webinar invites. This means you and your communications are likely to be considered spam and sent to a place that will get you blacklisted in more ways than one. There was a guy in Chicago who did this at practically every event in town and was on so many blacklists that I'd been warned about him repeatedly and weeks before I had even encountered him.

What do you do when you encounter someone like this? If they shove their card at you, go ahead and accept it so that you'll know to keep an eye out for them in the future, but don't feel like you need to give them a card in return. Just smile and say thank you, but if they ask for a card, and you don't want to give them one because you know nothing about them or how you might be able to collaborate with them, just say, "I'm sorry, but I'm almost out and I have another event to go to,"—which at some point you will—smile and move on.

Don't Be a Hit and Run

Make an effort to stay in touch or in occasional contact with folks you meet with whom you want to stay connected. Make notes on the back of the business cards they've given you about what they need help with or what their interests are. Then try to continue to pay attention to things that matter to them. This is the way to create quality connections and trusted new contacts.

For example, after you have followed up with a new acquaintance, and are now perhaps linked on LinkedIn, when you notice updates or changes in their status, go ahead and message or email them to comment on their change. It might be congratulations if you notice a new job, name change (perhaps they got married) or maybe a promotion. Or, if you know they're looking for a new opportunity or hinted that they would be soon, it might be to offer a suggestion about a good job board you spotted in their field or to connect them to someone new you have met. And, if you see that a contact is traveling or moving to a new town, offer to connect them to whomever you may have a quality connection with there.

Also, be sure to reach out to people when you don't need anything. Networking is about creating, nurturing and building relationships, and they need care and feeding. The whole idea is about not waiting until you need something to build a network; it's about continually cultivating and engaging in that network. The wider your network, the more people you know whom you've worked with. This also implies that all these people know the kind of person you are and the work you do.

ACTION:

Notice or learn something new about 3 of your current contacts this week. Look at their personal or company website or online activities to see what they're up to and if you can offer encouragement or support or a congrats, do so. Be sincere though; don't just go through the motions!

Don't Waste Your Time

Remember, have a goal or goals so you don't waste your precious time and energy. Don't go to a networking event unprepared. As mentioned earlier, try to research the types of people who will be there, and the format of the event. Also, focus on making connections of quality, not quantity.

It's also just as important to disconnect from the unproductive or overly opportunistic and one-sided networking relationships you'll unfortunately come across. And, for the latter, often, just by association, you could attract more unwelcome attention or unwanted perceptions.

Don't spend any more time on connections you make when you recognize that there's a suspicious or questionable agenda, or they simply aren't reciprocating or paying it forward. Just move on, and whatever you do, don't take it personally. Today's economy has many people coming from a slightly desperate position, and it's best to just forgive their tactics and practice empathy when you can, but you also don't need to let others take advantage of you. Trust your gut and move on.

Like most folks I know, I'd much rather have someone, who's not interested in building a quality connection with me, come right out and tell me they want to meet my brother-in-law (BIL), the head of Engineering at Motorola. It's much better than them stalking my Connections list on LinkedIn, and then trying to reach him by dropping my name during a cold call or email. My BIL, of course, tells me about it, and then I have that person's eyebrow-raising methods reflected on me ("Nice friends, Sandy," he says). Not to mention that they will now likely have my bad mojo out there on them.

Please don't misunderstand. I recommend being an "open networker" in that you are open to helping people get what they are looking for; they just need to tell you what it is first and at least offer a two-way street if they can. I say be happy to connect with people if they manage to build a relationship through the getting-to-know-you process. Just don't let people "leverage" your contacts without your permission or take advantage of your generosity by trying to get for free what you actually charge others for.

ACTION:

Identify someone who is better than you at networking, and attend an event with him or her. And if you really want a good mentor (to your wingman), offer to pay their way to the event. Then watch the way they work the room, and their approaches. You will learn a lot by watching and listening and you won't be any different than the other 80% of people in the room, who aren't totally confident in their networking skills either.

6 What Do You Do After a Networking Event?

Giving connects two people, the giver and the receiver, and this connection gives birth to a new sense of belonging.
– Deepak Chopra

Always Be Sure To Follow Up

Often, the real value of a networking event is found as much in the follow up as in the active participation at the event. Be sure to keep any promises you may have made to the individuals you met. Perhaps you promised to email an article of interest or send an introduction email to a vendor resource to someone you've met. You may have invited someone to join you for a one-on-one conversation about the current list of organizations you're thinking of joining or just to have an opportunity for collaboration. Or, through your listening and questioning, you may have identified a good vendor partner for your own company's needs. Within a few days, give them a call, or write and snail mail them a hand-written note, or send an email with the relevant info or item included, along with a specific, targeted link to your or the promised website.

BONUS TIP: If your follow up is in the form of a thank you note for something you benefited from, or simply a "it was nice to have met you" note, unless they have asked for them, *do not* include more than 1 copy of your business card with it. It's presumptuous to believe that the receiver wants to refer you people when you haven't even established a level of trust with them. That's a great way to negate the sincerity of your thank you note.

Be sure to show respect for those you contact. If your roles were reversed, what would make you responsive to follow ups?

I also asked Sima Dahl to give me her tips on this topic. Sima says, "One of the most important things to do upon making a new connection is to demonstrate your professionalism, dependability and desire to network." She suggests that you:

1. Follow up promptly, preferably within 72 hours so the conversation you shared is still fresh in their mind.

2. Make good on promises. Whether you offered to make an introduction, share a resource or schedule time to chat, see it through. If you need more time, let them know.

3. Clearly state your intentions. Express your desire to stay connected in the hope that you can mutually benefit each other by sharing connections and knowledge; ask for what you need.

4. Lead by example. Take a moment in the next few weeks to add value. The simple act of forwarding an interesting article can begin to put things in motion.

Another helpful share from the Upwardly Mobile study came from an "elite networker" CFO:

"It's like a sales process. I pre-qualify when we first meet: do they impress me; do I want to be associated with them? Can we understand each other's business and specialty? Is there some synchronicity? Whether or not, I always follow up with an email during the week if not sooner (and in the email, introduce another person to them for synergy). If they respond well to the email, and/or provide something back, then I put them in my 1st tier contact list, otherwise in my 2nd tier."

To help make this even easier, and because of the 17,000+ emails I have access to, I thought I'd share a few follow-up examples, some good and some bad:

Good General Follow Up

From: mbella@internet.net
Date: Mon, Nov 17, 2008 at 10:38 AM
Subject: Hotel Info
To: sandy@belladomain.com

Hi Sandy,

It was sure nice meeting you and Keith on Saturday at the dinner. My mom and I couldn't believe we were there until 11:00—with good company you don't care what time it is!!!

I deleted the email with the hotel info, but here is the link from the website I mentioned: http://www.americantuscany.com/.

I know they are encouraging folks to visit in 2010.

I also attached "Tips for Tuscany" which I also found on the website. It is very informative, but a little overwhelming as well. I went to Italy last year for two months and just arranged everything on my own and found locals to be my language partners. I guess it would be good to have the formal teaching as well, and of course the scholarship assistance would be nice too!!!

I look forward to seeing you on Mercer Island and getting together for cup of coffee sometime. I am heading to your website now to check out Bella Domain.

Enjoy your day.

Ciao,
Maggie
206-555-1212

Bad Reaching Back Into the Archives of Contacts

Mike McLovin has sent you a message.

Date: 7/07/2009
Subject: catching up

Greetings! How are you?

What have you been up to? It's been a while!

I don't think we have talked since my wife and I were bitten by the Red Cross triathlon bug. Well, we were, and we lived to tell about it.

Other than that, nothing much. We are still trying to finish off our fundraising—that's sure to happen soon.

And I'm ready to leave McLovin Solutions...but first I have to find gainful employment—or just employment—but gainful would be nice.

Let's have coffee and bran muffins or something sometime. No more donuts for me! Well, maybe a few.

Let me know what you're up to.

Mike

The Good, The Bad, and The Deleted

Why is the first example good? It opened with some kind words and reminder about how we met, then she provided the info she had promised to, and even threw out the idea of getting together again.

Why is the second so bad? I hadn't had any direct communication with the guy in probably a year, and he is only a casual acquaintance at best (never met his wife), so asking how I am seemed odd (would I really just tell him that I had the flu for ten days and was now struggling with an underwater mortgage? And furthermore, would he really care?), and then passively hinting at the need for help with a donation, AND help finding a job...again. Not even an offer to buy me the coffee or the aforementioned bran muffin, so that he can properly fill me in on what his real agenda is, and then finally a close of "let me know what you're up to" which just doesn't read as someone really all that interested.

Would you be eager to reach back to this person? These are the types of communications that get archived or just deleted.

Let's Get Back to the Good Though...

Here's an example of sending an opportunity

From: Sandy JK/BD
Sent: Tuesday, September 18, 2009 9:03 AM
To: Michelle Davis
Subject: Re: Equity Focus - September 2009

Hi Michelle, hope you had a nice Labor Day weekend. Thought you might like to contact this reporter to share your re-branding story...could be some good free press for you. As a PR/marketing type, I'm on a listserv where I receive these types of opps daily, but don't know the writers personally. See below...Sandy

Summary: Recently Re-Branded Your Company?
Name: Anonymous
Category: Business & Finance
Email: writer@email.com (Put RECENTLY RE-BRANDED YOUR COMPANY? in sub)
Title:
Media Outlet: Anonymous
Specific Geographic Region: N
Region:
Deadline: 03:19 pm EASTERN - 19 September
Query:

Looking to hear from small business owners/entrepreneurs who recently rebranded their company logos/packaging.

Especially interested in hearing from those who originally designed their logo themselves or had a bad experience with an amateur designer, before seeking help from a professional designer. What motivated you to opt for a professional design? What impact is your new look having on your business? What advice would you offer other entrepreneurs who are thinking about rebranding their company's look?

Send in your story/tips, before and after pictures of your logo (optional), and a brief synopsis of your company for consideration.

Thanks!

From: Michelle Davis
Date: Tue, Sep 18, 2009 at 4:06 PM
Subject: RE: Equity Focus - September 2009
To: Sandy JK/BD

Sandy,

Thanks! I appreciate you thinking of me! I also subscribe to HARO but don't always get to read them each time they come out!

I hope you're doing well!

Best,
Michelle

Michelle Davis - JD
Managing Attorney
Equity Focus Law LLC
(formerly Small Business Solutions LLC)
1800 108th Ave NE, Suite 200
Bellevue, WA 98004
Phone: 425-555-1212
Fax: 866-555-1212

Good Introduction Emails for Two People That Haven't Met

From: Peter Harris<peterh@email.com>
Date: Fri, Feb 13, 2009 at 1:50 PM
Subject: Sandy, meet Neil (and vice versa)
To: Sandy Jones-Kaminski, Neil Best

Hey Neil,

Ever since you graciously lent your insight to Moodio, I've been waiting for some way to reciprocate. To that end, I want to introduce Sandy Jones-Kaminski, a biz-dev wiz and uber-connector. Jeff Davis and I worked with her closely for most of last year, and she continually impressed me. As I was looking over your website, it struck me that Sandy might be a phenomenal resource, either to you or your clients.

Sandy, Neil used to be the Director of Product Management at Teamstar, and my first assignment there involved working with him closely for several months. It was a great experience that taught me a lot. Neil was one of the smartest people at Teamstar, and I have to say I enjoyed working with him more than just about anyone else.

Just wanted to connect two people I respect a lot, hoping it helps everybody in the long run.

– Peter

From: Sandy Jones-Kaminski<sandyjk@gmail.com>
Date: Tue, Mar 17, 2009 at 6:36 PM
Subject: connecting the 2 of you
To: Marcela Vorel; Kim Casault

Hey ladies, by way of this email, Marcela, one of my fav graphic designers, meet Kim, and Kim, one of my fav website pros, meet Marcela. If you check each other's profiles on LinkedIn & sites out, you'll likely see why the 2 of you should possibly offer to be referral partners for each other, but if not, no worries either. Sometimes folks I connect don't see what's truly possible immediately or their plans have changed, but most of the time it's pretty obvious.

Happy Connecting!

Best,
Sandy

Marcel Vorel
http://www.linkedin.com/in/marcelavorel

Kim Casault
Integrity-Driven Web Professional
http://www.cruxwire.com | My Profile on LinkedIn

Good Introduction of Two People That Need Each Other

This is an example of an email intro for a new connection I made at one of my PIF Party networking events:

Subject: Terry please meet Joan re: LinkedUp advertising

Hi Terry, by way of this email please meet Joan Smith. Joan's a friend and is currently contracting on-site at Macrosoft, and looking for an intro to someone that can talk to her about LinkedUp advertising. I knew LinkedUp's been working with areas within Macrosoft already, so I was fairly certain you could help her or would be able to direct her to someone on your team. I've supplied you both w/each other's contact info below, but don't hesitate to let me know if I can help in any other way.

Cheers,
Sandy

Joan Smith
w: 425/555-1212
m: 818/555-1212
jsmith@email.com
http://www.linkedup.com/in/jsmith

Terry Laird
Vice President, Advertising Sales
LinkedUp Corporation
Office: 415-555-0001
Mobile: 650-555-1212
tlaird@linkedup.com
http://www.linkedup.com/in/tlaird

BONUS TIP: Should you decide you want to connect in-person with a new contact, and are the one extending the invitation, be sure to at least offer to pay for their coffee, lunch or first cocktail. In the many conversations I have with people about networking, or what some folks call "brain picking" sessions, this is definitely one of their biggest pet peeves. Oh, and before you meet, do your homework on them or their business, especially if you need their help. Most people find an informal connecting meeting a huge waste of time if it starts with the dreaded question, "So, Samantha, what can you tell me about Acme Enterprises?" Especially when it's all there on a website or within LinkedIn.

A word of caution: Many people resent those who appear from nowhere and want to pick their brain. But some offer that they would be impressed if the person had at least read their blog, and then maybe commented or submitted one of their posts to a social media site or even sent them something relevant to their business.

ACTION:

Draft your own version of a follow-up email, and before sending it to any new contacts, send it to a few trusted friends asking for feedback on succinctness and sincerity.

Chapter 6: What Do You Do After a Networking Event?

7 When Should You Stop Networking?

Networking is marketing. Marketing yourself, marketing your uniqueness, marketing what you stand for.
– Christine Comaford-Lynch

Never. The bottom line is, people usually need to get to know you to feel comfortable enough to hire you, refer your business or share their valuable connections. They also need multiple exposures to you, in order to remember you when they hear of an opportunity, whether it is in person, by phone or via email. Once you get that new job or major client, you should not stop networking, because not only are there more opportunities awaiting you out there, but life can also be incredibly unpredictable.

As a case in point, in January 2006, after having a successful career in IT and business strategy, Jason Alba found himself unexpectedly in the job market, which was supposedly at that time a "job seeker's market." Jason quickly found that a job seeker's market does not mean the job search will be easy or short. Frustrated by the lack of real tools for job seekers, he decided to move forward on a tool that allowed a job seeker to manage and organize a job search (including what to do with all those business cards you collect). As the months passed, and as Jason learned the importance of networking, he incorporated a major networking piece into what is now known as JibberJobber. While JibberJobber was designed by Jason during his first real job search, this shifted its focus from a tool just to be used during one job search into a tool to be used to manage job transitions and network relationships during your entire career. Not surprisingly, Jason had really hit a nerve because JibberJobber became the foundation of his new and current career. If you want to learn more about JibberJobber you can check out Jason's site at http://www.jibberjobber.com.

In Case You Need Another Reason to Network

The effective networker study I mentioned earlier by Pepperdine University and Upwardly Mobile Inc., actually quantified the value of a quality professional network. The full name of the report is, "Professional Networking and its Impact on Career Advancement: Study of Practices, Systems & Opinions of High-Earning Professionals."

They designed the study to answer these questions:

- Do high-earning professionals in top positions know something the rest of us don't?

- Do they behave differently, invest in themselves differently and work with a different set of tools?

And according to their research, the answer is "yes." Elite networkers, defined as individuals earning more than $200,000 annually and holding positions of VP, CxO or higher, do something differently—and that something is what they call The Networking Habit.

Key findings include:

- Networking drives professional success

- Effective networking can lead to dramatic increases in income

I found loads of great info in the study and especially loved that these folks actually defined the **skills** associated with having a strong professional network. They include:

1. Maintain ongoing contact with key networking members
2. Proactively build relationships with mentors and advisors
3. Identify, research and add new connections to your network
4. Get meaningful introductions to key contacts important to your career success
5. Proactively create connections within your network
6. Evolve relationships from "contacts" into close connections

And according to the research, 70% of executives credit networking for their current jobs (compared to just 16% who credit job listings). And most aren't even networking well—75% said that they spend fewer than two hours per week on networking and focus on the wrong things.

If you'd like to get a copy of the report, you can find: Professional Networking and Its Impact on Career Advancement at http://www.upmo.com/knowledge/recent-research.html.

And if you'd like to find out if your network measures up, you can take their free Network Readiness Evaluator at http://www.upmo.com/profiler.

Try Getting Excited About Networking!

Some days you know you have an event to attend, but you're just spent from a long day of who knows what, or maybe you're questioning whether you have the energy to put on your extrovert face at all. Well, if you think about making progress on your own goals and contributing to your community via the stance of offering help to others first, you can embrace the fact that you're doing good things in the universe. That usually perks anyone up, and remember, almost everyone enjoys speaking with folks who are upbeat, excited and who show they are genuinely interested in them. You can show people you're interested in them by asking good questions and "actively listening." Remember to initiate the interactions, rather than just responding, and when you're asked what you need help with, you can easily move into the "I'm looking for" role in order to enlist help with your own goals.

I often encourage people to look at this pay-it-forward style of networking as a form of giving back or volunteering work, which can make this a "feel good" activity for anyone.

Here's yet another excellent blog post written by Matt Youngquist of Career Horizons (http://www.career-horizons.com) which speaks directly to the idea of focusing on the good feelings you can create as a result of effective networking. As I said earlier, Matt really knows his stuff:

Be the "Santa Claus" of Intangibles! (June 9, 2009)

In my blog entry a few days ago, I praised Liz Lynch (author of Smart Networking) for her wonderfully simple advice to those job hunters (and other folks) who want to be reciprocal in their networking efforts, but feel they just don't have all that much to give, at least of a tangible nature. Her advice? When all else fails, you should focus on giving people a feeling that they'll enjoy, cherish, and remember.

Maya Angelou once made a similar observation, which a good friend of mine recently reminded me about. Ms. Angelou remarked: "I've learned that people will forget what you said, people will forget what you did, but people will never forget how you made them feel."

Do these statements hold true in your own life? Can you cite instances of where somebody did a good turn by you, however small, that made your day and impacted you in a positive way you'll remember for the rest of your life? I know that I do. And if you don't, boy, I'm not really sure what to say. All I can assume is that you must be wired pretty differently from the rest of us....

So if you're a professional in transition, trying to master the subtleties of the networking process, I'd urge you to heed the above thoughts and observations carefully. In my experience, they represent one of the most significant realizations that can help a person take their networking efforts to an entirely new level, both in terms of their short-term job hunting prospects as well as their long-term career success. In all likelihood, after all, you're going to be rubbing elbows with hundreds of different individuals throughout the course of your search. And the one thing all of these people have in common is that they're human beings—and few human beings have a maximum upper threshold in terms of how much appreciation they enjoy receiving, as long as they perceive it to be genuine in nature.

So while it can be hard to think beyond your own immediate wants and needs during the turbulence of an employment search, you should strive to develop your "giving" muscles and focus on ways that you can consistently uplift and raise the spirits of those around you. Do you routinely go out of your way to make the people around you feel respected? Important? Appreciated? Entertained? Special? Helpful? Or that they've made a difference in your life or job search? If not, it's never too late to learn, since there are a near-infinite amount of ways that you can impart these feelings to people and the good news is that they're all free—or nearly free, depending on the gesture.

On that note, here's a list of some simple and proven techniques you can add to your networking repertoire, until you develop your own signature methods:

- Remember people's names and use them often. (Was it Dale Carnegie who said our own names are the sweetest music our ears ever hear?)

- Send a handwritten thank-you card expressing genuine appreciation for the person's time (this display of gratitude never gets old).

- Surprise somebody with a LinkedIn endorsement, a letter of recommendation, or another form of written testimonial (not just a nice gesture, but a potentially profitable one for the other party, as well).

- Make a thoughtful, relevant introduction on somebody's behalf (tell a person you're proud to have them in your network).

- Point out the qualities you admire in a person (don't overdo it, of course, but sincere flattery can get you everywhere at times...).

- Pass along a book, article, CD, or some other small token gift that you know a person will enjoy (shows you listened to what they like and care about).

- Make a donation to a person's favorite charity (if not immediately, then down the road, when asked, without hesitating).

- Put a person's advice to good use and then circle back around, a week or two later, with an update (home run! home run!).

- Express genuine appreciation for people's time; don't act obligated or entitled to their assistance (sadly, this behavior still stands out; I can't tell you how many contacts of mine have told me they've been "stood up" by other people lately who asked them for their help).

- Give the gift of your full, undivided attention (as above, it's sad that this gesture will differentiate you from others, but trust me, it will).

- Offer to return the favor, however possible, down the road (shows that you recognize the value of what you were given).

This is just the tip of the iceberg, folks. There are so many other examples I could share of where savvy networkers have found imaginative and inexpensive ways to make a person's day and make themselves "memorable" for all the right reasons. In fact, if you yourself have been the recipient of any such gestures, I'd urge you to submit a comment on this posting and share your story with the rest of us. Speaking for myself, I know that I can personally recount dozens of people who have made a lasting, positive impression on me through some small gesture or the other, over the years, and that these people hold a "special status" in my life/business sphere that money alone could never, ever buy.

Nothing liberates our greatness like the desire to help, the desire to serve.
– Marianne Williamson

Get Involved in Something

If you haven't joined at least one association connected to your company's industry or your potential future industry, you absolutely positively need to. Most of these groups hold loads of events, and just being a member of Rotary or something like a local tech association is great, but also think about targeting groups where your future area of interests will be piqued or your expertise will stand out and/or be valued. It'll be a completely different experience. Think: Big fish, small pond here.

For example, if want to move from accounting into professional project management, join the local or regional chapter of the Project Management Institute and start meeting people via their online groups or at their events. Or, maybe you're thinking about getting out of the corporate rat race and going back to school to get a coaching certificate? Well, join or volunteer at the local chapter of the Society for Human Resources Management and start connecting with folks that might be able to refer clients to you in the future.

In the don't-waste-your-time vein, I advise really getting involved with some of the groups or associations you have joined or have been thinking of joining. Try to attend their gatherings regularly because this conveys reliability and provides the opportunity to reinforce new relationships. By volunteering to do things you are willing and able to do, your dedication, competency and service will be clearly visible and set you apart. Plus, by putting some time in, you will naturally build quality connections to leaders and influencers in the group by way of the experiences you share and the side-by-side projects you work on together. Most organizations eagerly welcome volunteers who are reliable and willing to work, even when they are new.

In the words of one of the SVP level "elite networkers" mentioned in the Upwardly Mobile study cited earlier:

"I maintain active involvement in organizations such as rotary, little league, alumni associations, church...any place where people gather to talk and exchange ideas. Residual benefits come from working on a particular social or charitable issue together—if people see you are involved and have common interests, then they're drawn to you. People like to work with like-minded people, so business tends to come from that."

As you fulfill your commitments, group members will likely develop trust in you, and often be more than willing to help you. Boy, talk about some quality connecting! When you work shoulder-to-shoulder with others in a volunteer capacity, the vibe is totally different. Plus, you'd be surprised how little of a time investment most professional volunteering actually requires. Don't use your fear of not being able to give enough time as an excuse to not get involved. If you do, you'll miss out on developing quality connections or trusted relationships with people with whom you want to network. Besides, today so much help or participation happens online or via phone, so it's never been easier to make good impressions or grow your social capital.

If you're not familiar with the term social capital in this context, it refers to connections within and between social networks. Having social capital supports the belief that "it's who you know," as well as "what you know" that makes a difference in your life and business or career. It is a term originally associated with sociology concepts. Today, it speaks of the resources such as information, ideas or support that individuals are able to acquire by virtue of their relationships with other people. Basically, social capital is the quality and quantity of the relationships you've built over the years.

Clearly, it is important to keep cultivating your network, and once you land in a new job or secure a few new clients and people start emailing you, respond to them. Don't ignore them because you still need to maintain your network once its usefulness is not as urgently needed by you. Don't fall into the habit of not maintaining your network. There's a lot of activity you can do that tends to fall by the wayside but shouldn't, like staying involved in industry groups and attending conferences. Ignoring these opportunities until it becomes an emergency again won't help. Once you have a network going, you need to keep it active. Some day, you'll need it again.

ACTION:

Check the local event calendars for upcoming networking opportunities and add them to your calendar at least a month in advance. As the date gets close decide if you'll attend or not and sign up so you can start doing your research. Social Domain (http://www.socialdomain.com) is a really good one for the Bay Area, Washington DC, Chicago and Los Angeles, and you can also try your local business journal or chamber of commerce sites. See the Appendix A for some additional suggestions.

8 Effective Networking—It's in the Details

Keep smiling—It makes people wonder what you're up to.
– Bob Dolfay

Remember the Details

If you're at a live event and nametags are supplied, be sure you put it on the right side of your chest. The right side is the *right* side (that's how you remember it) because it provides an easy sightline and synchs with your handshake, which, yes, should be firm. We've all experienced the too hard or too limp shake, so please don't be one of those people. That's not a good way to be memorable.

Always have a *smile* and some type of business or personal card ready to offer people at all times. And, yes, a pen or pencil can come in handy as well.

BONUS TIP: If you make your own business or personal cards using something easy and inexpensive like VistaPrint (http://www.vistaprint.com), be sure your cards are the type on which you can write with a regular pen. Another big pet peeve out there is not being able to write on the back of too many of the cards currently in circulation. Many people like to make a note about what you're looking for or how you're connected on the back of the card you give them.

Try to find your own networking inspiration or look to create you own style because, as mentioned earlier in this book, my adopting a paying it forward approach to networking was validated and further inspired when I read about the concept described below:

NetWeaving—"Good things happen to people who...*make* good things happen."

That is the slogan of the Bob Littell, the founder of NetWeaving International, and what some people call the "BUSINESS version of Pay It Forward."

Bob brilliantly espouses that "It's not about getting someone to send you referrals, it's all about putting other people together, and you are the referrer."

For more information on the concept of NetWeaving, please check out Mr. Littell's website at http://www.netweaving.com and the Pay It Forward Foundation at http://www.payitforwardfoundation.org.

A Few Things That Can Go Wrong At a Networking Event

Besides being on the receiving end of the aforementioned nametag scan, or a business card commando, there are quite a few things that can throw even the most seasoned pro for a loop while networking. For example, I once attended a women-only event in Chicago that, to be perfectly honest, I will admit to having had serious reservations when I first heard about it. And sure enough, I had one of my most favorite lame duck experiences ever. Yes, another rule—trust your gut about an invite, especially if you're not 100% sure about the person inviting you.

This particular lunch event had one of those awkward change-your-table-at-the-next-course requirements, and after I finished what was my second elevator speech recital, where I explained that I had just moved back to town after being in San Francisco for over 4 years, and that I was looking for full-time or contract opportunities where I could help with marketing strategy, business development or channel sales, I was rather sarcastically asked by a small biz CPA, "Can you explain that again? You channel sales? From where do you channel these sales?" as she looked up to the heavens and rolled her eyes. Now maybe she asked this in this way because I had mentioned San Francisco, and she definitely looked like someone who may have spent some time hanging out in "The Haight" in her youth, but clearly she had never heard of sales channel development and assumed I was talking about using metaphysical tactics to help clients get sales. Not quite.

The lesson I learnt that day was to seriously consider your audience whenever you are among mixed company and try to tailor your message accordingly. In fact, it's best to have a few different versions of your intro, so you don't sound like a canned radio announcer while delivering it.

In closing...

I believe that networking can be a fun and easy way to enrich your life, contribute to your community, broaden your horizons, and enhance your career or business. But, I also believe that it can be potentially devastating to your social capital and personal brand if you act rudely, insensitively, or don't do what you say you are going to do. It is crucial to your success that you treat networking as an exchange of ideas, information and experiences. And, remember, in networking, reciprocity is key, so be generous in sharing your talents, knowledge, and ideas, and always be respectful of and demonstrate appreciation to those around you, whether they appear to be able to help you out immediately or not.

Once you get even more comfortable with your networking, you'll probably start chatting people up in line at the DMV, in coffee shops, elevators, at parties, on airplanes, and, well, just about anywhere. It's all great practice, and you just never know where your next quality connection will come from. And, please feel free to join my Bella Domain Networking Group on LinkedIn or Facebook to share your success (or funny) stories there. I'd love to hear them!

9 How to Have Your Own Networking Event

Since one of my goals for this book is to encourage others to take networking into their own hands, I have supplied a bonus chapter titled "*How to Have a PIF Party*" which contains the how-to's for having your own networking event.

A few years ago I recognized that there had to be a better way to make and cultivate quality connections, so I started having what have become known as "PIF Parties."

I was inspired by an approach from a business referrals oriented concept, and then chose to give it a name that most people recognize as being focused on helping others, either with or without their knowledge. PIF means to pay it forward, and at PIF Parties, that's what people do.

Introduction

After moving to Seattle, Washington, by way of Chicago, Illinois, in November 2005, I'd say it took well over a year for the impact of a local phenomenon called the "Seattle Freeze" to become apparent to us. During that first year, our level of enthusiasm for our new town was very high, and it took quite some time for the magic spell of the "Emerald City" to be broken. However, once it did (and from what we've experienced, to newcomers, it always does), we were not about to pack up and skip town or become discouraged and withdrawn like so many non-natives to the area unfortunately do.

Instead, we took matters into our own hands, and started having events that only attracted what I started calling "anti-freeze types." These are people who are affable, open and genuinely eager to engage with others.

Combine the above with the "give me" or "what can you do for me?" behavior demonstrated by too many people at the majority of the typical networking events I was attending (unfortunately, this is not a Seattle-only phenomenon), and I was more than ready to start hosting an event called a PIF Party. That's PIF, as in pay it forward. A PIF Party is a usually free event with first-name-only nametags and lots of friendly, helpful people.

Wouldn't you like to be at or associated with an event where all the folks attending have arrived with the intention of offering help to others first? And, if you're curious about what good comes from doing this, since I began hosting PIF parties back in November 2007, loads of great PIF stories have been shared. A few outcomes have included:

- New business opportunities created

- Job candidates recruited

- Elusive introductions made

- Deals closed

- Re-connections to long lost contacts

- Jobs found

- New subscribers to blogs

- Doctor referrals

- Learning (Facebook explained)

- Volunteers recruited

- Cleaning services found

- And even a few dates for some single people.

As you can see from the list above, hosting a PIF Party can result in many different types of positive outcomes. The best part is, you and your guests will feel great at the end of the event because, even if you personally didn't experience a PIF moment at the party, all you need to do is think about how many you maybe have helped create.

My hope is that, after reading this bonus chapter, you'll become motivated to have your own version of a PIF Party soon.

What Exactly Is a PIF Party?

The general theme of the event is that each guest comes to the party with the intention of simply offering help to someone else first. And, as can be expected, at the end of the event, each person leaves not only feeling good about having offered help to others, but also feeling grateful for the help they themselves may have received.

The help could be personal (need a tip on a car camping location near water) or professional (want to find a mentor outside of your company, need clients or employees for your business) or maybe even spiritual (looking for a yoga studio on the west side).

How Do I Plan and Host a PIF Party?

Start by putting a list of emails together of people that you have either recently enjoyed meeting or with whom you have already had positive experiences. Keep in mind that you can invite people who are as yet unidentified as being generally PIF-like, but as the PIF phenomenon continually proves, if they're not PIF types, these folks will likely weed themselves out by simply not attending.

NOTE: My rule is if people don't bother to RSVP to the invite, but I can see that they've been lurking (viewing the online invite usually more than once), they generally don't make it on the next invite list. I also tend to remove people that say "yes," and then don't show, and never offer an explanation after the event. Also, depending on my gut about the person, I may do the same if they replied as a "maybe," but then also never explained. I think bad social skills are the bane of our existence and not rsvp'ing illustrates a general lack of good manners. I would prefer not to support such bad behavior, and besides, it just doesn't support the spirit of what PIF is all about.

Lastly, for the first invite, I do not turn the option on that allows attendees to invite others, because for the first gathering, you are the person more-or-less vouching for the attendees. After folks have attended at least one PIF event, you can then allow the PIF types to invite others they are ready to vouch for at the event.

The first invite to a PIF Party went out via an online email invitation system (evite) and said this:

For the last year or so, I've been thinking about gathering a group of like minds to connect with on a regular basis. Between my desire to simply stay in touch with some of the awesome people I've met since moving here, as well as the need I have to help others see what is possible, it was a no-brainer that I start some sort of regular get-together. It then became just a matter of when....

The when became obvious once I realized I was starting to drain my cash reserves from having all my get-togethers around coffee, lunch or drinks. And then also as I started talking about doing this and loads of y'all starting asking to be part of it.

Therefore, the when is now and I'd like you to consider this get-together the precursor to what I'm hoping will become know as:

PIF - Seattle: you come to the gathering with the intention of helping someone/anyone other than yourself.

From these parties, my intention is to form my own (or help some of you form) what might be called:

A Mastermind Group—a team of like-minded people who come together regularly to help support one another's goals.

I'm inviting you to be part of this initial gathering to determine whether you'd like to participate in such future events.

Please RSVP to this invite and I'll look forward to seeing you at the first get-together.

Follow-up invites have looked like this:

Some of your emails and current events told me it's time for another PIF Party!

*As many of you know, Bella Domain's PIF Parties have become one of the ways I stay connected to folks I meet. Please feel free to use them in the same manner **if** the folks you'd like to invite are pay it forward type people just like you!*

We are going to meet at Bob's Sandbox in Belltown again. It's located at 3219 4th Avenue/Seattle, WA 98191/206.555.1212. The folks there have been pretty accommodating and most of the feedback received on the venue, food and parking has been good, so we're sticking with a sure thing.

Please use this invite to include a friend or two because this 5th PIF Party is definitely open as long as your guests are folks who are willing to offer help to someone else first.

Looking forward to seeing you there!

Suggested donation: Since this is a no-host bar event, you need only bring your willingness to help someone else. Well, that, and an appetite, since if you get there before 7:00 they have a great small plates special.

*P.S. Another reminder that you need not be shy about asking others **if** they need help. Even if it appears you can't help them, it's always nice to be asked, and sometimes when we get asked what we need, we can get so excited that we forget to ask the person who asked us! :-)*

Another invite looked like this:

 **Pay It Forward Party**

Ready for PIF Party #6?

This time around, I am paying it forward by having this month's PIF Party at an awesome new venue in the South Lake Union neighborhood of Seattle. It's called Smoot Nook Center and they are hosting a Happy Hour-Open House and we're all invited! They are located just east of Eastlake Ave and north of Davis St. Please see http://www.belladomain.com for more venue information.

Hope to see you soon and definitely bring along some new pay it forward types, if you've met any since the last party. I have and am! :)

*P.S. Another reminder that you need not be shy about asking others **if** they need help. Even if it appears you can't help them, it's always nice to be asked, and sometimes when we get asked what we need, we can get so excited that we forget to ask the person who asked us what they need. **Please** don't be **that** person.*

How Many People Should I Invite to My PIF Party?

This is entirely up to you and the venue you choose. The invite usually goes out to about 60 people, and then 30 RSVP "yes" or "maybe," and then about 10–15 usually show up. This size has turned out to be ideal because it makes it possible for most attendees to meet the others, and allows for some productive conversations to take place.

Where Should I Have a PIF Party?

Pick a place in a part of town that either works best for you (you are the host and ringmaster, after all!), or that is convenient for the majority of the folks who will likely attend. Are most of the "yes" people city folk or is it more of a suburban crowd? Choose a location with the commutes in mind.

I had the first PIF Party in my building's party room, which was okay because use of the room was free, but we bought food and drink as if we were entertaining in our own home, and most of it sat uneaten (it's hard to talk with your mouth full), and was impossible to use as leftovers during the following week (how much cheese can *you* eat in a week?).

Instead, pick a grown-up bar or restaurant (food available with drinks is best*) with a decent-sized bar and call ahead to give them a heads up that you are planning to meet 10–15 friends there. Typically, they'll accommodate your group with its own section and be prepared for lots of separate checks.

*I always recommend a place with food because a PIF event is not a slosh 'n josh par-tay, and they typically start right after business hours and wrap by 7 or 7:30 p.m. Folks can always continue on elsewhere for dinner, drinks or whatever else, once the party wraps up.

What Do I Need to Do As the Host At the Party?

Have a table or section of the bar set up with a few felt tip markers, stick-on nametags (be sure you get the kind that actually stick...don't skimp and try to use mailing labels as I once did), and a fun, possibly, seasonal assortment of stickers for folks to use to give their nametag some personality, a.k.a., flair. Nametags are best with first name only, and a sticker (or 2) of their choice.

Greet as many people as you can when you first see them, and then, just mingle around as much as possible so as to set the example for the other attendees. Your goal should be to ask as many folks as you can what they need help with and be willing to answer that question yourself.

For some rather pleasant reason, attendees appear to like to be able to offer help to the host.

NOTE: Prior to the first few parties, I completely forgot to think about this and had a deer-in-the-headlights look on my face when asked. I've since learned to think about my needs the week before and have my "ask" ready. Once it was the car camping question, another time it was "subscribers to my blog updates," and recently it was able-bodied volunteers for a friend that had a rushed meeting room set up for an important event she was facilitating.

How Does a PIF Party Actually Work?

A PIF Party is really no different than when a group gets together at someone's home, a wedding or their company's open house event. An easy way to start chatting in any of these situations is to start a conversation about something you know you already have in common, like the event itself or the person(s) hosting.

Recommended initial party chat in almost any situation goes like this, "So, how do you know Sandy (insert host's name here)?" It's usually pretty easy to start spotting topics to continue with or questions you can ask from there, but at a PIF Party, at some point, you're encouraged to soon ask, "So, Stan (see nametag), what do you need help with these days?"

Ideally, Stan eventually gets around to then asking you the same question, but maybe he doesn't because someone else joins in the conversation, which is fine too. Just be sure you try to reconnect with Stan later at the event or give Stan your card (or a slip of paper with your contact information) and indicate that you'd like to continue the conversation, if possible, because you want to learn what it is he currently needs help with.

Also, when/if another person joins your conversation, be sure to share what you've learned or shared with Stan already, so you keep the conversation momentum going.

How Often Should I Host a PIF Party?

In order to build up some demand, I recommend hosting a PIF Party every other month. I can usually tell when it's time to get one on the calendar because emails start coming in and people start asking me the date of the next one. Every other month also allows you plenty of time to meet and invite some new people in between the events.

In closing, it's best to just relax and trust your instincts about people at this special event, since most folks invited to a PIF Party have a pay it forward way about them, so you'll be in good hands and have lots of fun to boot!

If you'd like to learn more or engage us to help you plan and facilitate your own version of a PIF Party, you can reach me at sandy@belladomain.com or via my website at http://www.belladomain.com.

ACTION:

If you plan and host your own PIF Party, please email me to let me know how it went!

Additional Resources

Here is a starter list of sites to find local business networking-oriented events:

Social Domain Local Events Guides in San Francisco, Washington DC, Chicago, and Los Angeles. Categories include: Arts, Business, Gala/Benefit, Lecture, Literary, Performance and more:
http://www.socialdomain.com

The Seattle Networking Guide - a guide to community groups, events, and calendars for professional, civic, and social networking:
http://www.iloveseattle.org

Social Media Club Seattle's community calendar:
http://smcseattle.com/calendar

Seattle's Technology News Source:
http://www.techflash.com/events.html

Xconomy delivers valuable content through a global network of localized (Seattle, Boston and San Diego) blogs, events, conferences, and other initiatives designed to connect people and ideas:
http://tinyurl.com/ygcokzl

And then, if you do a search on "networking events Chicago" for example, you'll come across sites like:
http://www.networkingmonkey.com/
http://www.networkinchicago.com/

Of course, don't forget about local Meetup groups in your area. Meetup is a network of local groups. They make it easy for anyone to organize a local group or find one of the thousands already meeting up face to face. I did a search on Business Networking in my zip code (98040) and 318 events came up!
http://www.Meetup.com - here's an example:

http://business-referral-networking.meetup.com/cities/us/wa/seattle/

Your local Chamber of Commerce and Business Journal both usually do a good job of culling business-oriented events.

For example:

Under Chamber Services/Business on little Sebastopol, CA's Chamber of Commerce site I found this:
http://www.sebastopol.org/business_networking.html
http://www.northphoenixchamber.com/
http://tinyurl.com/yfypkax

Event listings or calendars can also be found on most trade association websites, as well as industry trade journal sites.

The American Marketing Association offers:
http://www.marketingpower.com/Calendar/Pages/default.aspx

American Society for Quality:
http://www.asq.org/networking-and-events.html

Executive Women International:
http://www.ewiseattle.org/default.aspx?name=calendar

Networking, Business, and Social Events for Philadelphia Professionals:
http://www.networkinphilly.com/

Other resources include:

Eventbrite helps businesses and organizations of all sizes manage, promote and sell-out their events:
http://www.eventbrite.com/

Net Party Business and Social networking events for young professionals:
http://www.netparty.com/

Twitvite is an event manager tool that helps you organize Tweetups and make meaningful connections through social media:
http://twtvite.com/

Use Eventful to find, share and promote events:
http://eventful.com/ - do a search on "business networking."

Socializr is a web service offering free online event invitations, and innovative ways to share event information:
http://tinyurl.com/yg2pf2j

The Online Guide to UK Networking:
http://www.findnetworkingevents.com/

Biznik is a national, but localized community of entrepreneurs and small businesses dedicated to helping each other succeed:
http://biznik.com/

Do it yourself Social Networks from Ning, for example:
http://www.ning.com/search/networks?q=business+networking

Books:

Here are some books currently available that can't hurt, and definitely might help you develop your networking muscle. I've read quite a few of these and the others came highly recommended:

'Never Eat Alone: And Other Secrets to Success, One Relationship at a Time' by Keith Ferrazzi and Tahl Raz

'The Tipping Point: How Little Things Can Make a Big Difference' by Malcolm Gladwell

'Dig Your Well Before You're Thirsty' by Harvey Mackay

'Emily Post's The Etiquette Advantage in Business: Personal Skills for Professional Success, Second Edition' by Peggy Post and Peter Post

'Smart Networking: Attract a Following In Person and Online' by Liz Lynch

'I'm on LinkedIn—Now What???' by Jason Alba

'I'm on Facebook—Now What???' by Jason Alba and Jesse Stay

And, keep an eye out for the forthcoming book titled, 'Sway Factor: The Art of Networking in a Digital Age' by Sima Dahl.

About the Author

Sandy Jones-Kaminski is a self-described net-working enthusiast and an accomplished business development professional. In 2002, Sandy launched her own partnership marketing and biz dev strategy consulting practice called Bella Domain, LLC (http://www.belladomain.com). Prior to becoming an entreprenuer, Sandy led the strategic partner program as an executive director and regional sales manager for TriNet, an HR business process outsourcing company based in Northern California. In that role, Sandy was responsible for managing business development programs with partner sales teams and channels. Previously, Sandy was also a VP-level operations executive within the business intelligence arena. First at Information Resources, Inc., and then at Strategic Media Research, both in Chicago. She is also a recent VP of Networking for one of the

largest chapters of the American Marketing Association. With more than a decade of experience in business development and partner/client relations for SaaS and business services companies, Sandy knows how to make meaningful connections, cultivate relationships, host some great networking events, and create what she refers to as good "social capital." She can help you or your team with everything, from developing a networking or business development strategy, to getting value out of online social networking tools, to your own personal branding and social capital creation. Not surprisingly, Sandy's active on numerous social media sites, such as LinkedIn and Facebook, and enjoys traveling and exploring the world with her favorite person and traveling partner, her husband Keith Kaminski. You can connect with her directly at
http://www.belladomain.com.

Other Happy About® Books

Purchase these books at Happy About http://happyabout.info or at other online and physical bookstores.

JASON ALBA & JESSE STAY
Foreword by: Afterword by:
Lee Lorenzen   Robert Scoble

HappyAbout.info

I'm on Facebook—
Now What???

This book will help you come up with your own action strategy to get value out of Facebook.

Paperback $19.95
eBook $14.95

JASON ALBA
Foreword by Bob Burg

HappyAbout.info

Networking Online—
Making LinkedIn
Work for you!

This book explains the benefits of using LinkedIn and recommends best practices so that you can get the most out of it.

Paperback $19.00
eBook $14.00

42 Rules™ for Effective Connections

For anyone who wants to improve communication, get better results in any networking environment, and alleviate the stress and anxiety that comes from building a business where you have to go out to meet potential customers this book is a must-read.

Paperback $19.95
eBook $14.95

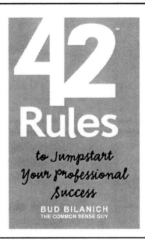

42 Rules™ to Jumpstart Your Professional Success

42 Rules™ to Jumpstart Your Personal and Professional Success provides the reader with practical, down to earth advice on how to create a successful life and career.

Paperback $19.95
eBook $14.95

Additional Praise for this Book

"Certain social networks see the world before the world sees their network, others are seen by the world and marketed to before they know what hit them, and still others have no clue of the world and the world could care less. This book shares how to be genuine yet strategic in your approach to building a network that matters and will last. It is hands on, buoyant and stitched together with Sandy's fun, pragmatic yet philosophical approach."
Aaron Fairchild, Managing Partner, G2B Ventures

"Undeterred by challenge, inspired by opportunity, and energized by collectivism, Sandy knows of whence she speaks in connecting the art of networking to the science of linkage theory: she's 'been there/done that.' And no one knows how to do it better...from making the entrance to working the room to managing the postscript. Once you read, no...once you internalize this provocative précis on human dynamics-the only question you'll be left asking is: 'now what comes next from Sandy Jones-Kaminski?' Stay tuned...."
Barron T. Evans, 'Terminal' Networker-Global Bridge-builder

LaVergne, TN USA
15 December 2010
208845LV00003B/13/P